The current US administration has identified the Lebanese Islamist group Hizbullah as a key threat and the group's media a source of increasing anti-Americanism. Secretary of Defense Donald Rumsfeld blamed al-Jazeera, the leading Arabic language news station, for encouraging Islamism by broadcasting beheadings of hostages in Iraq, a charge the station denies.[1] In President George Bush's State of the Union address in 2004, he focused on Arab television stations he claimed are responsible for "hateful propaganda" against the US. The stations distort news and show explicit images producing anti-Americanism.[2] Al-Manar, a satellite television service launched by the Lebanese Hizbullah, is one of those stations. The US maintains that al-Manar is anti-Semitic and promotes hatred, and lists Hizbullah as a terrorist group.

To counter what is viewed as the promotion of anti-Americanism, hate and terrorism, the administration banned al-Manar from American airwaves in December 2004, though legally, the basis for banning the television station was due to its role in aiding Hizbullah, not its messages.[3] The US launched its own television station, Alhurra, to compete with messages from Arab media outlets in general. Are these efforts likely to succeed, winning the hearts and minds of Arab and Muslim TV watchers? To answer this question, an analysis of Hizbullah's appeal is necessary. What messages is the station actually carrying, and with which constituencies do they resonate? How does banning the station affect their credibility? I analyze al-Manar's ideology and link it to its bases of support. I then examine the American actions to counter this ideological influence, and how those attempts are received in the Arab world.[4]

In contrast to previous reports of al-Manar's broadcasts, my study did not find overt support for suicide bombings or attacks on Americans or Israelis. Most coverage was comparable to other stations. The basic character of the station mainly comes through in the spots, fillers between programmes, which highlight negative American policy and military actions in the Middle East and the power of the resistance (Hizbullah) to protect Lebanon against incursions. Al-Manar has recently moderated its more extreme rhetoric, with the goal of increasing Hizbullah's presence in Lebanese domestic politics, as interviewees claimed. Indeed, research for this study was partly conducted during the period of parliamentary elections in Lebanon. If moderation has progressed with political participation, the finding is far-reaching, demonstrating a non-confrontational method of mitigating an organization's radical stances.[5]

Al-Manar's stance can be interpreted as the frames or messages of a social movement, geared to encourage attitudes which spur action and involvement. These messages centre on Palestine, the continuing threat posed by Israel, American bias in the Arab-Israeli conflict, the power and importance of community solidarity, and pride in Arab culture and the achievements of the Islamic Resistance (Hizbullah's armed wing), which have strong resonance in the Arab world. Alhurra's message is intentionally opposite to these and is interpreted as another element in the western siege against Arab culture. As such, its presence adds to the polarization of Arab and American messages and perspectives. Ironically, messages communicated on the station are increasingly rejected as propaganda. Viewers watch Alhurra to identify the American spin, while they follow al-Manar to learn the dangerous truths banned by the Americans.

The Problem: Hizbullah and al-Manar's Media Ideology

Hizbullah was officially established sometime between 1982 and 1985[6] as an umbrella group uniting religious Shi'a groups in Lebanon in the wake of the Israeli invasion. Its military wing is called the Islamic Resistance. The group benefited from significant Iranian aid, military and

financial, and advocated the establishment of an Islamic state. To this end, during the Lebanese civil war Hizbullah utilized suicide bombings, and is accused of sponsoring or undertaking terrorist actions in the early 1990s in Latin America. The organization is officially listed by the US as a terrorist organization. While they are pro-Iran, they are anti-Taliban and anti-bin Laden.[7]

After the end of the Lebanese civil war, Hizbullah transformed itself into a domestic political party, and is now viewed as legitimate by Lebanese of all confessional stripes. Debates over the Ta'if accords resulted in forsaking the goal of an Islamic state and cooperating with other religious groups and parties in Lebanon.[8] Hizbullah has participated in elections in truly democratic fashion, allying with other religious groups, including Christians, and encouraging its members to vote for them. Its social service provision and anti-corruption stance have strengthened its base of support among all groups. The party currently holds 14 seats of a 128-member parliament.[9]

Most importantly, the withdrawal of Israel from Lebanon in 2000 due to Hizbullah's attacks on Israeli soldiers in the south, and the concomitant disbanding of the South Lebanon Army funded by Israel, was seen as a unique event demonstrating the power of the group and its commitment to Lebanese sovereignty. Many Lebanese leaders agree that disbanding Hizbullah's militia, now numbering only a few hundred paid soldiers, is not an urgent priority, although they would like to see the militia disarmed. The group itself maintains that its resistance helps to prevent incursions into Lebanese territory or meddling in its affairs. Israeli occupation of the disputed Sheb'a farms is cause for the continued existence of the resistance armed forces. Arabs repeatedly refer to Hizbullah's victory: it is responsible for Israel's only forced military withdrawal from the territory. The group's resistance role has earned it acclaim in the Arab world, which elevates its tactics as a model to emulate. Further, this role has tamed much of the historical animosity between the Sunni and the Shi'a, the Shi'a having long been viewed as a heterodox sect. For its part, Israel views Hizbullah as a prime adversary, despite the group's currently limited domestic role.

Some observers maintain that Hizbullah suffered a crisis of identity when Israel withdrew from southern Lebanon because the movement lost its key issue and rationale. This conclusion is misplaced. The centrality of Palestine and concern for specifically Lebanese domestic politics were key issues prior to the end of the civil war and the Israeli withdrawal in 2000, but they became increasingly prominent with those two events. Further, both these concerns enable Hizbullah to broaden its image to include other confessional groups and increase its following in domestic electoral politics. Featuring the Palestinian-Israeli conflict and the potential for Israeli incursions underscores the group's chief accomplishment, the successful resistance against Israel in southern Lebanon. Rather than experiencing an identity crisis, Hizbullah simply altered the emphasis in its relations with Israel from liberation to protection of Lebanese land.[10]

Indeed, neither the group nor its constituency is single-focused.[11] Hizbullah has specifically national concerns (what is termed Lebanonization) and its own foreign policy priorities. While Hizbullah remains relatively close to Iran, its ties to the country both ideological and material have diminished since the end of the civil war. Globally and nationally, the organization is focused on securing a place for Shi'a, who have traditionally been marginalized and repressed. With its successful resistance against Israel, Hizbullah has effectively mainstreamed the Shi'a, creating a greater acceptance of them by Sunnis than ever before. Previously, the Shi'a were viewed as passive in their widespread political exclusion and economic repression. Hizbullah's advocacy of resistance altered the image from victim to equal by seeking political empowerment based on communal solidarity and pride,[12] an ideological change pioneered in Lebanon before the civil war by Musa al-Sadr.

Domestically, the organization is popular for its provision of social services, in stark contrast to the Lebanese state's lack of provision for the poor. These services are furnished to all those living within areas where the organization functions, regardless of confession. Politically, Hizbullah maintains a developmentalist, pro-poor ideology. Like other Islamist groups, corruption is one of its main themes. Hizbullah lobbies for more services from the government, and highlights the lop-sided reconstruction of the country which is overwhelmingly concentrated in the rich areas outside the reach of the poor. The counter-demonstration by Hizbullah after Prime Minister Hariri's assassination, in response to the one focusing on the Syrian occupation, was held in the expensive, reconstructed downtown area to underscore the differing assessment of the country's priorities.[13] This pro-poor and anti-materialistic theme is communicated by al-Manar and appeals to a wide swathe of the public that cannot afford the upper class lifestyle widely promoted in Beirut. That lifestyle is also viewed as promoted by international capitalism and the US, making its rejection one of the main perceived differences marking the boundaries of the other.

Hizbullah's other main focus is the Palestine-Israel conflict. Particularly after the Israeli withdrawal and the advent of the second or al-Aqsa intifada later that same year, Palestine has become an increasingly central focus of the organization. The group appeals to the Palestinian refugee camp population, who have strong practical incentives to ally with the Shi'a group. On a practical level, Hizbullah views the Palestinian conflict as an opportunity to expand its base of support.[14] It seeks to recruit among the Palestinians, and use their numbers in its competition with the other major Shi'a party in Lebanon, Amal. The Palestinians, who are overwhelmingly Sunni, have been drawn to Hizbullah's concern with Palestine. Their status in Lebanon is increasingly insecure and they are searching for a place within the country's closed political and social system. To this end they have begun to differentiate themselves from the general category of "foreigner", which includes Filipinos,[15] and embrace the previously-rejected category of refugee as a bargaining position for civil rights.[16] Further, tens of thousands of Shi'a Palestinians from southern border villages were naturalized in 1994, counter to the government's widely broadcast position against naturalization or *tawteen*. A number of Sunni Palestinians were then naturalized, presumably to maintain the sectarian balance.[17]

The Palestinian cause resonates in the Arab and Muslim worlds, particularly in the absence of any country to defend the Palestinians or resist Israel, outside of Hizbullah's success in southern Lebanon. While al-Qaeda used Palestine as a mobilizing issue to unite its disparate Arab Afghans in the international sphere, Hizbullah's use of Palestine has domestic roots and uses. The movement was officially announced on the anniversary of the 1982 Sabra and Shatila massacre, in which civilians from two Palestinian camps in Beirut were killed by a Christian militia under Israeli army cover.[18] The central theme of Palestine and Jerusalem resonates not only among the Shi'a and Palestinians in Lebanon, but with the Sunni population more broadly. Its continued use grants Hizbullah further legitimacy, and allows it to expand its domestic constituency.[19] As a result, with its Shi'a base and support from many Sunnis, Hizbullah is now widely accepted by the Lebanese population. Ninety-nine percent of Lebanese Muslims view

Hizbullah as a legitimate resistance[20] and the 8 March 2005 demonstration after the assassination of former Prime Minister Hariri fielded between 600,000 and one million demonstrators in support of the party.[21]

The theme of Palestine also unites Lebanese across confessional lines. Fairouz, the famed Lebanese singer, has numerous popular songs about Jerusalem and Palestine. Lebanese Christians, while harboring no affection for Palestinians themselves, also feel the power and pull of the loss of Palestine, and 74% of Lebanese Christians view Hizbullah as a legitimate resistance. The Lebanese Army used its one semi-successful battle in the 1948 war against Israel's formation, the battle of Malikiyya, as the foundation myth serving to unite the many confessions. The power of this battle turned the armed forces into a national institution, from its origins as a colonial army, and created a collective identity to prevent fragmentation during most of the civil war.[22] In the first decade of Lebanese independence, when Muslim and Christian military cadets were so divided as to be unable to agree on a name for their class, a tradition upon graduation, they could agree only on one – the name of "Palestine."[23]

Al-Manar

Hizbullah began its television station al-Manar in 1991 broadcasting only locally in Lebanon. In May 2000, al-Manar began transmitting by satellite. Al-Manar is generally available throughout the Arab world on satellite, and in Lebanon over land. The station is banned in Europe and the United States. The station now has bureaus and correspondents around the world, and is most famous for its broadcasts of Hizbullah attacks on Israeli soldiers in southern Lebanon. Polls list al-Manar as one of the top four news stations in the Middle East.

To date, the main research on al-Manar was done by Avi Jorisch of the Washington Institute for Near East Policy. His work emphasized the station as a terrorist one, dangerous to the US and Israel, overtly teaching and promoting terrorist techniques and airing anti-Semitic and anti-American messages. Jorisch concludes that the station's core mission is to promote terror, hatred and radicalism. Unlike al-Jazeera, he states, there is no redemptive value to al-Manar's coverage; it is undiluted propaganda, wholly dictated by its militant funder, Iran.[24] He claims that the station is active in the incitement to violence, providing video instructions of suicide bombing techniques.[25] Broadcasts during the months al-Manar was studied here did not confirm such instruction programmes.

While based on research, Jorisch's work is polemical and alarmist, drawing conclusions not supported by the data or lacking contextual knowledge of many of the references. For example, Jorisch jumps to conclude that al-Manar does not air commercials on its satellite version because advertisers desire to hide their support of the station from the "prying eyes of US-based viewers".[26] A lack of context is apparent in his assessment of one phrase used by the station, "Jerusalem, we are coming," which he interprets as a threat. The line actually comes from a well-known song by Fairouz, about religious unity around worship in Jerusalem as a city of peace.[27] Jorisch had extensive access to al-Manar's officials and programme directors, an openness they now regret, as Jorisch subsequently led the international campaign against al-Manar. Station officials are now wary of interviews and researchers.

Al-Manar is funded by Hizbullah, and though precise costs or amounts are not known, one source put the annual cost of running the station at $10-15 million.[28] Funding from Iran dropped dramatically after the end of the civil war and the death of Ayatollah Khomeini. Meanwhile, Hizbullah has increased its revenue from non-Iranian Shi'a and Lebanese sources. Revenue comes from expatriate remittances, donations and tithes. (As a religious party, Hizbullah receives tithes of one-fifth of income from its constituents.)

Al-Manar must be placed within its domestic and regional context. Lebanon has numerous television stations, each with its own ideological stance. These stations proliferated during the civil war, creating more than 50 land-based stations. That number decreased after the war to a dozen or so, of which only have satellite capability.[29] When al-Manar was licensed, the government simultaneously granted a license to a Christian religious evangelical station, Télé-Lumière, to maintain a confessional balance in the country's media.[30] Unlike commercial stations elsewhere, Arab satellite television does not generally subsist through its advertising. Stations are politically geared and funded. Particularly in Lebanon, each major political trend has its own station, which at times the leader personally finances. Revenue from advertising does not generally cover expenses, a condition true of many Lebanese television stations.[31] While ads are of secondary importance, they do serve a purpose. They indicate the market where the station is popular. Most ads on Arab satellite television are aimed at the Gulf market.

Al-Manar relies particularly little on advertising. A station with a mix of global and local supporters, like al-Manar, is theoretically attractive to advertisers. However, the station reportedly turns down 90% of potential advertisers due to their violation of its standards. It will not accept commercials for alcohol, tobacco, or ones in which women are presented as objects for sale or temptation.[32] Further, advertising on the station is less attractive to Gulf advertisers for political reasons, since the Shi'a are seen as a distinct community separate from the Gulf one.[33] Until 2004, ads were broadcast only on the land-based station, not the satellite. Among their advertisers were big American and European companies. A scandal brought this to the attention of the US Congress, which accused the companies of aiding terrorism, and the American and many European advertisers withdrew their commercials.[34]

Currently, ads on al-Manar are infrequent and few, airing mainly in prime time. They are local and regionally-based. On the land-based station, ads are for local clothes, shoe and toy stores, along with other retail stores and a Lebanese cellular phone company. Several manufacturing companies advertise cleaning detergents, air conditioning products and food products of European origin. On many of these, non-veiled women are shown. In addition, the station airs announcements for social service organizations and schools run by Hizbullah, computer and sports classes, summer school and Quran classes. There are even fewer commercials on the satellite version. Local advertisements are eliminated and only ads for basic food products, cleaning and air conditioning goods were observed during this research.

Broadcast Coverage

Al-Manar[35] (Lighthouse) is one of the top stations in the Arab world, seen as enacting a new version of politically independent media.[36] At the 8th Cairo Television and Radio Festival, al-Manar won the most awards of all the competitors. The Lebanese Media Group, which includes al-Manar and al-Nour radio (also Hizbullah affiliated) won four and nine awards respectively.[37]

The station identifies itself as "qanat al-muqawama", the station of the resistance, and has been labelled "resistance media" by one Arab editor.[38] Some of al-Manar's programming, particularly promotional spots, as expected, decry Israel, emphasize the right and ability of the Islamic Resistance to defend the country, and highlight flaws committed by the US. But the remainder, the majority of the station's air time, is generally unbiased. Indeed, much of the programming is educational and modernizationist, and finds parallels in western public broadcasting such as PBS. The station's ideological stance includes promoting a public role for women within an Islamic framework, advocating for the poor and moderate in income, emphasizing community solidarity, lobbying for government social services, and solidifying the place of the resistance and its fighters in Lebanese society.

The content of the station's broadcasts has not remained constant but evolved along with Hizbullah's political position and opportunities for participation in the Lebanese government. With the prospect of gaining a cabinet position with the 2005 elections, the station's more extreme rhetoric became muted. Differences between the satellite and land-based coverage have decreased as al-Manar and Hizbullah sought to broaden their appeal to non-Shi'a communities and to solidify their political position in Lebanon.

Further, the station has won acclaim by not limiting its interests to its own confessional group. According to an official at the Lebanese Ministry of Information, al-Manar has a strong community following, perhaps the strongest, because the station hosts interviews of persons from all political trends and confessions. Al-Manar remains neutral in these "Crossfire"-type programmes, he stated, in order to increase its viewership. These shows are key to the station's attractiveness. Al-Manar compared favorably to other stations which merely advertised their own political viewpoint, excluding alternative trends from airtime.[39] The religious aspect of the station is not overt compared to other religiously-affiliated stations, according to most audience opinion. Religious explanations and discussions are minimal. Al-Manar reiterates its religious identity mainly through broadcasting the call to prayer, and like other stations includes more religious programming during Ramadhan.

Entertainment programmes or serials are of short duration, as is common in the Arab world, often only a few dozen episodes. The channel purchases and airs inexpensive Egyptian and Syrian serials, many historically oriented, about life during Ottoman times. Another series, "'Ashna wa shufna," is a comedy typical of other Arab stations. One, for which the station received fierce international criticism, focused on the Jews in history, called *The Diaspora* or "al-Shattat," and contained factual inaccuracies.[40] This was a Syrian-made drama that the station said it purchased quickly without viewing the entire series in advance. Whether this is true or not is less important than the station's realization that airing the series was a mistake.[41] Other well-liked programmes deal with historical issues, such as the programme on Mary, the mother of Jesus (Sitt Maryam).

Numerous programmes seek to educate, showing scientific interviews on meteors and geology, new technology from the US, and "Discovery"-style programmes on animals, which focus on the needs of the constituency, cow milking technology for example. Spots on Arab countries and their history are frequent. Some of the programming is public service-oriented. A spot announcement promoted obeying the law – "Do not go against the law".

Palestine

The station is clearly centered on Israel and the Palestinians, including extensive coverage of Israel's actions, a stance consistent with what observers have described as Hizbullah's preoccupation with knowledge about its adversary.[42] It is perceived to be speaking out for the Palestinians, the "underdog," against the Israeli oppressor, and airs events and viewpoints not seen on other stations.

Al-Manar helps to break the myth of the Israeli army's invincibility and resurrects the idea of resistance for the Arabs.[43] Hizbullah military operations were broadcast, covered by al-Manar reporters "embedded" with them. These episodes of Israeli troops killed in southern Lebanon were initially shown on al-Manar,[44] and aired on Israeli TV only later.[45] To reinforce its victories, mainly for its own constituency, the station's psychological campaign "Who's next?" shows Israeli casualties and a blank space for future soldiers.[46] The station broadcasts some spots in Hebrew, aimed at demoralizing the Israelis. Arguably, this programme affects the group's Lebanese constituency more than it does the Israelis, providing evidence that Hizbullah is indeed active in combating the enemy, even on the media front. By promoting Hizbullah's accomplishments against the Israelis, al-Manar fulfils a fundamental task for a successful social movement, convincing its members that success is possible. Indeed, Hizbullah created a feeling of victory in the Arab world, shared by Christians and Muslims alike, that translated into popularity for al-Manar.[47]

Viewers seeking news on Palestine turn to al-Manar. Some observers assert that the station's broadcasts are crucial to the sustenance of the intifada.[48] However, two indirect factors could be construed as aiding the intifada. First, al-Manar's reiteration of Hizbullah's success against the Israelis can be interpreted as a model for others to follow, as indeed it has been throughout the region. Second, the station focuses much of its news and entertainment on Israel and the Palestinians. News and interviews come straight from the Palestinian territories and feature Arab perspectives on events rather than Israeli. Interviews include those in Islamist groups such as Hamas, leading observers to conclude that al-Manar is serving as a voice for terrorism. Another reading would be consistent with the view of al-Manar as an opposition or resistance media, covering the non-dominant perspective.[49] Other programmes highlight the historical actions of Israelis, seeking to uncover their crimes and terrorist actions, such as the Spider House, Terrorist-Zionist Crimes, and others.[50] Information and interview programmes focus on the Palestinian right of return in international law.

Since the Israeli withdrawal in 2000, the station's emphasis has switched from fighting Israel to supporting the Palestinians and protecting Lebanon (and the Shi'a) by resisting future Israeli incursions. Spots imply that resistance means being watchful, thus Hizbullah is the vanguard of protection for the sovereignty of the Lebanese state. Spots on the station highlight the resistance activities, demonstrating Hizbullah soldiers in hiding watching the border with Lebanon. "Bil-mursaad" (In the lookout) states that no one can approach the border without being detected; a bird is shown getting near the border, it is trapped, and then the remains of soldiers' uniforms are seen. Another one reiterates that 425 resolutions attempted to get Israel out of Lebanon: one resolution succeeded in getting Israel out – *al-muqawama* (the resistance). In another, a woman is shown sleeping at night, another woman sitting next to her baby sleeping in the crib. All eyes are sleeping, but there are eyes watching out for your safety – the eyes of *al-muqawama*. One spot states, amid dramatic music, "al-quds fi khatr" (Jerusalem is in danger).

Some spots equate the resistance's protection with the protection of Lebanon ("himaya al-muqawama, himaya lubnan"). One spot states that in this time, we are all responsible for our brothers and community – do not forget the martyrs and resistance fighters. Another touts the resistance as safety for the generations. Others tie the culture of the simple, traditional Lebanese people to support for the resistance. A spot shows children playing, men smoking arghileh (water pipe), women cooking in traditional pots, and Lebanese celebrations before showing the resistance. In another, an Israeli is shown killing people, while old men and Hizbullah soldiers resist. The messages and ideology mirror those used by armies in other parts of the globe, touting the suffering of the soldiers on the citizens' behalf, the respect due to soldiers, and soldiers' own self-respect and pride earned through military service. Other segments recount Israel's incursions into Lebanese and Arab soil, and Hizbullah's responses. The station broadcasts celebratory spots to its martyrs, Imam Hussein, and occasionally Ayatollah Khomeini. Award ceremonies for injured fighters who completed job retraining are also shown.

The Israeli-Palestinian conflict is highlighted in al-Manar's lighter "human interest" programming as well. Game shows such as al-Muhimma (the mission) are centred on contestants seeking to enter Jerusalem and answer historical questions mainly on facts to do with Israel and other resistance organizations. In two series (al-'Aidun and Yatathakkarun), Palestinian elders recount oral histories, telling stories of village life in the homeland.[51] Another programme reunited a Palestinian family who moved from Beirut to Gaza with the members of the family who stayed in Lebanon. Along with pictures and direct interviews, the interviewer discussed how the individuals remember their family, family stories were recounted, and they discussed the pain of *ghurbeh* (being far away) and the feeling of *hanin* (nostalgia) for family.

News Coverage

Daily broadcasts begin with the news and a review of the headlines in differing papers across the ideological spectrum. This type of coverage is common on Arab stations. In news, the station emphasizes events in Iran, Palestine, Iraq and US foreign politics. There is a clear anti-Israeli bias. Jewish interests are seen as powerful in determining US policy and electoral outcomes. Israel is viewed to be behind the banning of al-Manar in France, and American reports from the Congressional Research Service are used to support the assertion of AIPAC (pro-Israeli) and Saudi funding of American elections. Potential threats against the Arab and Muslim worlds are reported. The station communicates the idea that Israel is hegemonic in the region, tightly connected to the US, and that Israel and the US want a weakened Lebanon and Syria, unable to resist Israel's actions. Iraq was targeted to fragment the country, not make it sovereign.

Al-Manar follows American domestic and foreign politics closely, with a special interest in the Arab world. Regarding US positions on Lebanon, one spot states, "This is how the US deals with UN resolution 1559" (calling for Syria to withdraw from Lebanon), while depicting a man holding a large wooden stick the size of a bat, tapping it hard against his hand, menacing and ready to strike. This is followed by another scene, with the words "and this is how the US treats UN resolutions regarding Israel". The screen shows a man picking the petals of a daisy and states: it applies, it does not apply, it applies, and so on. As in alternative reporting in the west, the Bush administration is seen as anti-Muslim, and Christian Zionists as behind much of those policies. The station distinguishes between Christianity ("true" Christianity) and the actions of Zionist Christians. Regarding the US presidential elections, the station's position was that no difference among candidates existed. Bush and Kerry shared an American strategy, while their methods might differ.

News reports from Iraq are clearly opposed to US action there: "the American occupation army". Actions against the Americans in Iraq are reported and resistance in Fallouja is followed closely, along with terrorist actions against the Iraqi people by the resistance there. The latter are depicted in all their tragedy. Details of torture, indictments and alleged rapes by American troops are reported, and more importantly, the station quotes American media reports regarding those issues. Further, while the US emphasizes the threat facing it in Iraq to mobilize domestic support, al-Manar spins this same fact as a positive, demonstrating the power of the opposition.

In addition, al-Manar programming highlights any mistakes or faux pas of the US. It emphasizes that Guantanamo and Abu Ghraib are not being discussed in the US nor are those responsible punished. Lawsuits and problems about the Pentagon that are reported in the US press are carried by the station. Importantly, American moves to correct problems are also reported, such as the Congressional meeting to research events at Guantanamo Bay. Flaws in the US are emphasized, such discrimination against blacks, the American Indians, and slavery in history. Spots and filler segments highlight negative actions of the United States. One historical piece, "WAR," focuses on US invasions of other countries. Another shows UN proposals favourable to Arabs, and a US veto on them.

In other foreign policy issues, Syria is praised for its support of Hizbullah's fight against Israel, and the relation between Syria and Lebanon is viewed as complimentary. The Saudis are condemned for not financially helping others and being corrupt. Religiously, differences between Sunnis and Shi'a are papered over as not consequential. The station's coverage of Iraqi elections was generally perceived as balanced, without bias for a particular candidate.[52]

Regarding Iran, the station cannot be regarded as merely a mouthpiece for that regime. After the new Iranian president was elected, the station like others, including Alhurra, focused on the question of how his conservative stance would affect policy. In particular, the question of gender relations was discussed. Interviewees refuted the idea that the new president would, or could, segregate the sexes in public. They stated that his record in office as governor of Tehran has not reflected such extremism, and civil society, including numerous women in parliament, is too developed to return to policies characteristic of previous harsh times.

Local Politics

In domestic politics, al-Manar stresses the Hizbullah ideology of developmentalism and the need for state services. It emphasizes unemployment, corruption, and the need to cross confessions and join together as a nation. No sectarian animosity was detected. On the contrary, Christians and subjects involving Christians were treated respectfully. This cross-sectarian character was noted in interviews. Town hall type programmes are also produced and aired by the station, such as Nafitha 'ala al-mujtama' (Window on the community). People gather and express their opinions on particular social problems and other topics.

During elections in Lebanon, the spots focused on the importance of voting and Lebanese unity. The elections were spun as an affirmation of democracy, a message to the US, counter to the interests of Bush, the US and Israel. "Your vote protects Lebanon," a spot stated ("sawtak biyahmi Lubnan"). Another spot advertised "wihda Lubnan," or one Lebanon. However, the power of the Shi'a community in Lebanese voting was reiterated, in both a get-out-the-vote perspective and one which sought to remind those elected of the Shi'a role in their victory.

Community solidarity and the need for cooperation are emphasized. In Ahl al-medina (the People of the City) people in a city were challenged to live alone for three days, without speaking to anyone, in order to win a prize. Not a reality show, the series was acted, with a clear moral point emphasizing community. Upon the announcement of the contest, all stores and schools closed. Everyone wanted to win the prize, so teachers left their posts and butchers closed shop. The city was paralyzed. The series demonstrated, in the style of an after-school special, that such a situation was unsustainable. After a few hours, the community decided that they could not live without a social life, and that no one would get the prize. The programme demonstrates the believed contrast between the individualism of the west and the Arab and Middle Eastern value of community.

Women and Morning Programmes

At least half of the announcers and programme hosts are women, all veiled (with the *hijab*, the scarf covering the hair). However, not all the women appearing on the shows are veiled, and commercials (on the local station) show women unveiled. Al-Manar states that it rejects all advertising which depicts women as objects.

Al-Manar shows health and household programmes that are popular and relevant. Mornings, after the news, are devoted to a weekly theme, usually geared toward women. One week discussed child rearing, how both mother and father have roles in child socialization. Professors discussed their psychological perspectives on the family and children. Another tackled the problem of what to do when a child does not want to go to school. Other episodes discussed plant arranging, summer fruit, and new women writers. One segment hosted a local clothes designer who utilizes intricate sequin patterns in her clothes.

The programme al-Lu'lu al-sagheera (The little pearl) documents a day in a woman's life, emphasizing the role of mother and teacher of her children. The programme shows how she manages to live frugally as a widow, how the children (two boys and two girls) are taught, their daily schedules, traditions, and the role of religion in daily life. She rejects commercialism and western culture, without it being mentioned by name, and stays away from Beirut, the home of much materialism.

In another programme, a seventeen year old girl envies the Christians she sees who dress well, have nice cars, and meet boys. Questioning and rejecting her own family's poverty, she obtains work in a boutique in Beirut. Her mother objects to this work, but she proceeds. She wears western clothes and does not veil. She meets a man and marries him. He becomes a strict Muslim and demands that she quit work and wear the veil. She does so, and discovers that her mother and the people of her village respect her again. She finds fulfilment and happiness, and obtains a job, sanctioned by the community, cleaning a school. Reunited with her mother and village, she blames herself for her lost time in Beirut living a western lifestyle. She takes religious classes and speaks to school children about her negative experience in Beirut amid the commercialism and materialism. In contrast to her position at the outset of the series, she expresses her gratitude for being a Muslim and for her humble life.

Segments of the programme Mashakel wa hulul (Problems and solutions), aired during Ramadhan, discussed difficulties a family could have and propose solutions. The segments aided parents in socialization tactics for their children, teaching them to keep their own problems away from their children, how to talk to children to prevent them from misbehaving, and emphasizing the importance of education for children, equating it to alleviating the suffering of the community. One segment discussed women's rights in Islam. Another showed children asking their parents to help poor families, as was done in the Prophet's times. A segment stressed the centrality of the martyr's children and their education, because they are seen as a role model for others.

Children's Programmes

Children's programmes are varied and appear to resemble public television elsewhere in the world. There are cartoons, computer-generated "Teletubbies"-style shows, and puppet shows that promote non-smoking. Other programmes for children include American movies such as Rain Man and Disney cartoons.[53] Some programmes are religiously-oriented. One game show centres around children's knowledge of the Quran. The show involves Palestinian and Lebanese children averaging 8-12 years of age, over half of whom were girls, competing to recite verses.[54]

Other shows for children focus on and reiterate the need for a resistance. Asdiqa' al-manar (Friends of al-Manar) is a game show set as a pretend war game, with youngsters 10-15 years old fighting with pretend weapons (guns, grenades, swords, arrows) against an enemy that appears western. It is understood that this enemy is Israeli. The children, Shi'a and Palestinians from the camps, shout, "God is great," as they cross over outdoor territory to meet the enemy across the bridge. The fighters maintain the moral high ground by enacting a form of brotherhood among the fighters, sharing their food, bonding with each other. The series Fatat al-muqawam al-Quds (Jerusalem Resistance Boy) involves a young fatherless boy (a recurring theme) who wants to find his father who went missing in a war. To do so, he learns to fly planes, starting with paper airplanes, then with flying school lessons. Unable to find his father, he joins the military – Hizbullah's Islamic Resistance – and tries to recruit his friends to join. Religion is not mentioned in the series. The boy's mother praises him, while she herself is depicted traditionally dressed, advising her daughters to stay clear of western influences and keep to the southern and rural areas instead. The village sheikh is not clearly Sunni or Shi'a, but is a voice of wisdom.

Response: Banning al-Manar and Launching Alhurra

The US response to al-Manar has been to ban it entirely from the US and to promote its own channel, Alhurra, to compete for Arab audiences.[55] The station was intended to move "the people of the region away from extremism and violence and toward democracy and freedom".[56]

Banning al-Manar

The campaign in the US and Europe to remove al-Manar from satellite stations began with an opinion piece in the *Los Angeles Times* in October 2002. The piece accused American companies who advertised on the station of promoting terrorism.[57] PepsiCo, Proctor and Gamble, and Western Union were cited as advertisers on al-Manar's local broadcasts (the satellite broadcast at the time was commercial free). This was followed by a letter to Congress to put pressure on these companies, using the opinion piece as support.[58] The advertisers pulled out, and pressure to ban the transmission of the station itself increased. At the same time, al-Manar was under siege in Europe. Having agreed not to air messages inciting hatred, the French Audiovisual Council granted the group a licence, with a warning to stick to its word.[59] However, it was indeed banned from French airwaves and European ones in general, followed quickly by an American banning of the station in December 2004.[60]

The immediate reaction of the banning of al-Manar in Lebanon was defiance. In response to France's ban, fifty cable operators in Beirut halted the French station TV5.[61] The Lebanese Minister of Information declared it censorship of any opposition to Israel, and students demonstrated in support of al-Manar.[62] The banning was criticized by Reporters Without Borders, who warned against confusing anti-Israeli positions with the fight against terrorism.[63] Al-Manar voluntarily stopped broadcasting several days before the ban was to take effect, a move that prevented other stations on the same satellite network from being removed from the airwaves as well. This action won the station praise from other networks and its watchers, fuelling the image of the station as sacrificing for others.[64]

The US's Alhurra

As a counter to the negative image produced by Arab media stations, the US stepped up and altered its participation in public media. A triad of new US media were launched in the Arab world: a satellite TV station, a radio station called Radio Sawa, and Hi magazine, which together are publicly funded through a half a billion dollar grant to the Broadcasting Board of Governors, producers of the Voice of America. Alhurra, or "the free one", is the commercial free satellite TV station launched on Valentine's Day 2004. The station itself was allocated $102 million start up funding,[65] $62 million for first year by Congress, and $40 million more for an Iraq-specific station.[66] Fifty-two million dollars were proposed for the station in 2005, and $652 million requested for international broadcasting in 2006. This includes the proposed expansion of Alhurra to European forums and the creation of a Farsi (Iranian) language satellite station.[67]

Alhurra is targeted at the general public, especially those under the age of 30, in contrast to previous US public diplomacy efforts which were geared toward elites.[68] Alhurra's broadcasting includes cooking and fashion shows, entertainment, geographic and technological programmes, documentaries and news.[69]

There have been complaints about the station from its beginning. The station's first guest was President Bush, who, according to some media observers, was fielded "softball" questions only. Other criticism is that the station has ignored topics of importance to Arab viewers. Breaking news is particularly problematic. Alhurra was broadcasting a cooking show when Sheikh Yassin was assassinated by Israel, and in contrast to all the Arab television stations, Alhurra remained with its original programming. The other stations switched to cover the breaking news. The station's director later admitted this was a mistake.[70] Similarly, the Cairo Khan el Khalili terrorist incident that killed three tourists was not covered for over an hour after other stations had switched.[71] These problems prevent the station from becoming a news source in times of crisis.

The station's news coverage is markedly different from that of other stations in the area. It does not air interviews with leaders of terrorist groups, such as the Taliban, in conformity with Congress's mandate.[72] Similarly, the station does not air negative aspects of the coalition presence in Iraq, or attacks on journalists, but will occasionally show the victims of terrorism. The spin of events also differs. People are not "martyred" but killed, and the station does not call terrorism "so-called terrorism" as other Arab stations do. Further, the common greeting used by Arab channels, *al-sallamu 'alaykum*, viewed as religious, is avoided in Alhurra, whose hosts instead say "welcome back".[73]

Alhurra relies heavily on western-produced and sub-titled programmes. Recently, it has begun to address this issue, adding more local material, including town-hall type debates and coverage specifically geared to the elections in Iraq, Palestine, and the US ("Iraq Decides, Palestine Decides, America Decides"). Alhurra's promotional spots emphasize elections and protest in the Arab world. One spot ends with King Abdallah of Jordan saying in English that "we" are making the Middle East a better place, after pictures of the Syrian President Bashar al-Asad and Syrian troops leaving Lebanon. Other spots show Iraqis voting and Egyptian and Lebanese protestors.[74]

The station's most popular shows are its non-news coverage, including travel, documentary, fashion, cinema and music programmes. It also has interviews with local fashion designers and writers. Hollywood events such as the Golden Globes and the Emmy awards are broadcast (live), along with baseball and football games to draw more male viewers. But the increase in such coverage is criticized by the Broadcast Board of Governors, the oversight body for Alhurra, since the station was intended for news. Mouafac Harb, the station's director, defends the fashion programmes, saying that people in the Middle East should see that there is a "grand and beautiful world" beyond their borders.[75]

For many critics, the station's limitations in coverage call into question its objectivity, neutrality and the basis for its credibility.[76] The lack of images of prisoners in the Abu Ghraib scandal significantly tainted the station's image. Interviews conducted by one writer in Lebanon indicated that not showing Palestinians' tragedies and Israelis as oppressors is a reason for not watching.[77] For some, Alhurra confirms that the US has embraced the promotion of propaganda more commonly associated with the dictatorial and Soviet regimes.[78] But according to Jon Alterman, Middle East Director of the Center for International and Strategic Studies, the presumption that information provided by the US government would be authoritative in the Middle East is flawed. The Middle East has long been used to government propaganda, and Alhurra appears as such to many.[79]

Alhurra is faced with what one writer described as an "existential" problem,[80] which results in the station either appearing to be the old-style government-sponsored propaganda, or evading Congress' dictates. It cannot be critical of the US due to its structure and organizational funding, but to effectively draw viewers from other stations for news coverage it must cover a variety of viewpoints as the others do, which inevitably involve criticism of US policies. Currently, the station treads the line between, partly since Congress is unable to directly monitor its broadcasts, which are in Arabic.[81]

The plethora of media alternatives complicates the question of what Alhurra adds. The station was intended by the US government to cover new and difficult issues presumably avoided by other Arab stations. However, Marc Lynch's recent research demonstrates that such an assessment of Arab television is false. Indeed, Arab satellite stations regularly cover difficult and presumably taboo subjects, including Islamist movements, torture in local prisons, censorship, corruption, women's rights, government repression, and economic problems such as unemployment and child exploitation.[82] In fact, this new coverage is heavily slanted toward self-criticism of Arab society.

My survey of Alhurra's content found it to be heavily weighted toward statements by American officials. Bush's speeches were covered extensively, occasionally taking up most of news broadcast time. Interviews with American officials about American events were translated and shown in Arabic. American military officials in Iraq were interviewed when events occurred in Iraq, and Israeli officials spoke on events in southern Lebanon and the Palestinian Authority. Reporting a clash between Hizbullah and the Israeli army in Southern Lebanon, newscasters stated that the Israelis knew it was coming, that it was not a surprise to them. This is important since the knowledge and competence of the Israeli army have been discredited by its unsuccessful occupation of the area. Coverage of the military skirmish focused on the Israeli side, showing Israeli soldiers preparing for war. Newscasters discussed the "message" that Israel was attempting to send. This contrasts with al-Manar's coverage of the same event which focused on Palestinians and the effects on them. Similarly, al-Manar's report on the clash between Hizbullah and Israel in southern Lebanon highlighted domestic effects. The perspectives of the two stations are diametrically opposed. In one, Israelis and Americans speak and act, they interpret news and events. In the other, Palestinians, Lebanese and Iraqis have voice and agency.

Shortly after the new Iranian president was elected, Alhurra's talk shows focused on the president and the specific questions of whether Iran is a dictatorship, even if it holds elections, and whether the extremism of the new president is Islamic or not. The station also focused on whether the new regime would alter arrangements between men and women in Iran, preventing them from sitting next to each other, for example.

Another talk show presented the difficult question of poverty in Morocco, and what caused it. Could corruption be the problem? No, the station's interviewer and interviewee concluded. Corruption could not possibly cause all of the poverty. The cause lay elsewhere. This is significant since corruption is one of the main themes of Islamist movements in the Arab world, including Hizbullah.

Conclusion: The Effectiveness of Countering al-Manar

Is banning al-Manar and promoting an alternative likely to increase support for and knowledge of the US? Banning al-Manar in fact promotes the idea that the station is airing news deemed unfit for American viewers, and in the process, inflates the presumed power of al-Manar and empowers it as an alternative to US views and propaganda. Promoting Alhurra enhances the credibility of Arab media, which are seen to be airing uncomfortable truths so dangerous the US has taken the trouble to counter them.[83] Further, the widespread view that al-Manar was banned due to pressure from Israel and pro-Israeli organizations discredits the United States' proclaimed neutrality and its democratic values of press freedom. This reinforces the sense of being "besieged" by a global Israeli campaign.[84]

Alhurra's problems begin with its name, viewed as condescending and inappropriate.[85] "The free one" assumes the traditional US stance of representing the better society and further contradicts its journalistic nature. Critics argue that it cannot be free if owned by the state. Alhurra has also been criticized for lacking cultural appropriateness, being unable to resonate with the audiences, and broadcasting without market research (or advertising) to determine audience reception.[86]

Audience and Viewership

Numerous sources cite al-Manar as one of the prime sources of news in the Arab world, particularly about Palestine. The top four news stations, which capture 70-80% of satellite viewers, are al-Manar, al-Jazeera, LBC (Lebanese Broadcasting Company) and Abu Dhabi TV.[87] According to the Jerusalem Media Communication Center, the majority of Palestinians watch al-Jazeera, Abu Dhabi, and al-Manar.[88] Jorisch reports a poll in 2003 which found those in Jordan turned first to al-Manar for news of Palestine (28%), followed closely by al-Jazeera (27.5%).[89] A lecturer in Cultural and Women's Studies at the Palestinian Birzeit University stated that she watches al-Manar to hear news of Palestine, when the Palestinian Authority itself is silent.[90] One man stated that the station represents the moderate Muslim – not extreme, but focused on issues close to the average Muslim's heart.

My interview data show that, although there is a major trend of individuals watching all news stations keeping in mind the ideological leanings of each, al-Manar audiences are largely determined by national community. This trend crosses religious boundaries in Lebanon, including Shi'a and Christian Maronites. Some refuse to watch al-Manar, rejecting all things religious, and these often watch the Christian-affiliated station LBC. Others are very attracted to the station, citing its good programmes. Some individuals state that yes, the station does air some extreme statements, but also many good points not found elsewhere. Many Sunni Muslims in Lebanon have differences with the station over al-Manar's close relationship with the Shi'a and the Da'wa party in Iraq. In the Palestinian camps, with few exceptions, al-Manar is widely popular due to its coverage of Palestine and news there.

In Jordan, the overwhelming feeling is that al-Manar shows the truth. Palestinians in Jordan have enormous faith in the station, particularly after Israel left southern Lebanon. Islamists in Jordan (Sunnis) are attracted to the news coverage. They remain, however, wary of the station's Shi'a character. The news they feel is varied in coverage, and the station honest in its identity: it blatantly proclaims its stance as against Israel and the US in Iraq. This is respected.

Poll results on Alhurra, as reported to Congress, show the station's apparent success. However, these conclusions are unsupported by wider data and other polls. An ACNeilsen and Ipsos-Stat poll claimed that 34% reported watched Alhurra in the week before the survey. They were not asked how much they watch or if they turn to the station during a crisis. This is particularly important given the viewing characteristics of Arab audiences, who watch numerous channels for limited amounts of time each, complicating conclusions about viewer patterns and ratings.[91]

Alhurra is broadcast only to the Middle East, and is less available than al-Manar. It is available in Jordan, Iraq and Egypt for those owning satellites. However, some satellite providers do not offer it and there is heavy pressure on them to keep the station off.[92]

Even accounting for the smaller possible viewing population, numerous surveys contradict the rosy poll results presented to Congress. A survey by Zogby International and conducted by Shibley Telhami in June 2004 across a number of Arab countries found that al-Jazeera and al-Arabiyya are primary news sources. None, in fact, gave Alhurra as their first choice for news; a small amount, 3.8%, picked it as a second choice.[93] These results accord with my results in Jordan of the station in comparison and negative contrast to Arab coverage (see below). A Palestinian poll found only 1.1% watched Alhurra, whereas over 58% viewed al-Jazeera, 12% al-Manar, and 10% al-Arabiyya. Gallup's poll concluded that 6% of Iraqis watched Alhurra in the previous week. A survey by the Arab Advisors Group found fewer Egyptians watched the station (3%) than viewed BBC World (5%) or the government's Nile News (9%). Al-Jazeera again scored 88% of the public in that poll, and al-Arabiyya in second place trailed with viewership of 35%.[94]

It is also important to note that consuming American media is not the same as accepting the American perspective presented. Audience polls indicate that around a quarter of Jordanians and Saudis do watch Alhurra at least once a week but it is not a primary source of news for them.[95] For Radio Sawa, an ACNielsen survey revealed that 11% of Egyptians 15 years of age and older and 40% of Kuwaitis listened once a week. However, whether these individuals' attitudes toward the US changed as a result, or if perhaps they listened out of a pro-US stance to begin with, was not addressed.[96] Another survey of satellite users in greater Cairo found that most viewers (over 64%) felt Alhurra was not trustworthy as a news source; college-educated viewers trusted the station a bit more than those with only a high school diploma.[97] In comparison, almost 86% felt al-Jazeera was trustworthy, and almost 67% felt CNN was trustworthy.[98] Tellingly, only 8% of Alhurra's small viewing public deemed the station's coverage could be trusted.[99]

The most common audience reaction to Alhurra in Lebanon is indifference. It is seen as just another station, in a populace that has long learned to identify the ideological bias of the station and adjust accordingly. Many have never heard of the station, or if they have, they find CNN more credible. In Beirut, Christians report that they like Alhurra, believing it is more reflective of their interests in the way that al-Jazeera is for Muslims.[100] Recent interviews indicate that for the majority of the population in the Muslim areas, Alhurra is "all but dead".

Street interviews in Cairo demonstrated that the predominant impressions of the station were either indifference or attraction to the fluff and public interest programming, not news. Some felt the channel was low quality; others compared it to their own state-sponsored media. Many were hostile. The majority felt the channel was boring.

There were a variety of other ambivalent to negative responses to Alhurra. Some viewers, I found in Jordan and Lebanon, watched it only to compare the news with Arab media coverage and determine the difference. My interviews in Jordan accord with one interviewee in the Cairo survey who asserted that the channel is viewed as Israeli. Another interviewee stated that, in his opinion, the premise that the channel would make Arabs like the US is flawed, since if that were the case, the popularity of US movies would have done the trick long ago. Another respondent believed that Arab governments should ban the channel.[101]

My interviews concluded that the opinion of the stations is determined largely by ethnic or national identity lines. Palestinians do not trust Alhurra, and if they do watch it all, it is to see how differently the news is presented and compare it to other stations. Throughout Lebanon and Jordan people overwhelmingly believe that Alhurra shows them what the US wants them to know. Young Iraqis living in Jordan have hope in the US plan for Iraq and therefore watch Alhurra to see the American point of view. Older Iraqis' opinions generally accord with Jordanians in this regard, and are not sanguine regarding their country's future. These views translate into perspectives on the television station. Some believed that Alhurra was attempting to impose and convert Arabs to American ideas. The few who had a positive opinion of Alhurra mentioned only the entertainment coverage or the cultural interview programmes.

The effect of satellite TV such as al-Jazeera and al-Manar is questionable. One study failed to find a correlation between satellite television and attitudes toward the west. In fact, the most critical attitudes toward the west came from those countries with the lowest percentages of satellite TV viewers. While only 26% and 58% respectively of Egyptians and Jordanians have satellite television, these populations were the most negative toward the west. Lebanese and Palestinians, 84% and 85% of whom have satellite television, were less critical.[102] In particular, the view of the conflict between the west and the Muslim world as a religious one, a view often promoted on satellite television stations, has not translated into like attitudes among the populace. The study reiterated the view that Arabs triangulate multiple media sources with their own pre-existing beliefs and values.[103] Arabs have long experience with state-owned media, censorship and propaganda. As a result, ironically, they judge the station by democratic journalistic standards: its separation from government.[104] The history of biased media has created a populace of critical viewers, distinct from patterns among many western audiences.[105]

Polarizing the Issue Space

Jorisch and others offer a number of recommendations that would further polarize the environment. They advocate isolating Hizbullah and al-Manar, and criminalizing anyone dealing with them and all countries where the station has bureaus.[106] Such actions would further polarize the Arab world, and add credence to "opposition" media such as al-Manar. In a globalized information technology world, perspectives that resurrect the besieged and victimized identities of Arabs and Muslims are impossible to eradicate. In the absence of al-Manar, another forum would develop.

The policy conclusions of this study counter those seeking either to promote Alhurra as a solution or who see nothing lost in its presence.[107] On the contrary, this study indicated that the presence of Alhurra sets up a counterpoint and identifies particular views as clearly American, making rejection of those ideas clearer and adoption of alternative ideas more accepted. Alhurra adds to the sense of siege currently in the Arab world, the feeling of being targeted by an American attempt to alter their ideas, culture and values. Ironically, proof is demonstrated in the launching of Alhurra itself.

The American offensive against al-Manar may prove to be counterproductive. The muting of al-Manar's extremism over time supports the alternative policy of engagement and political inclusion. Former Ambassador Rugh maintains that US officials should participate in existing stations, in effect entering the debate and creating dialogue among the players, not one-way monologues.[108] By denouncing those stations as anti-American instead, the US is sending a message that free speech is only allowed when it is favourable to the US.[109] Not only does this reinforce feelings of a double-standard on the part of the US, but it sets up the US station as a government-sponsored propaganda outlet with which Arabs are familiar and have rejected. An increasing number of Arabs reject anything merely because it comes from the US, with the American stamp on it; this transfers onto messages from Alhurra. Thus al-Manar has benefited from the presence of Alhurra, as opposing messages are deemed not credible and al-Manar increasingly trustworthy in comparison. Similarly, some argue that for the Iraqi elections to have an effect outside that country, they had to be viewed on al-Jazeera, not Alhurra.[110]

Al-Manar both represents the ideas of its audience and attempts to alter them, to spur the constituency to action. A part of this process is altering their self-concepts from victim to empowered and proud. Tactically, many of the emphases of al-Manar can be viewed as effective frames for mobilizing against a militarily superior enemy. Importantly, the presence of Alhurra bears witness to the effectiveness and power of Arab media, since they were so dangerous the US was pushed to legitimize itself, to defend itself against counter-claims.[111] This demonstrates the fallibility or weakness of the opposition (the US), a necessary ingredient in drawing recruits to a movement.

Alhurra cannot replace stations such as al-Manar. The two offer differing symbols and messages. Al-Manar promotes community identity, solidarity and a modest life-style. Alhurra demonstrates the extravagance of western capitalism. Al-Manar gives voice and pride to the victims, and shows victory against an enemy. Alhurra's interviews are from the point of the view of that enemy, rubbing salt in the wound, as it were. Al-Manar does not conform to stereotypes of it (or of Hizbullah) that it marginalizes women or injects religion in all its programming. On the contrary, the station highlights practical problems of women and solutions proposed by them. The overwhelming majority of children's, entertainment, scientific and technological programmes are identical to those on any other station, American or otherwise. Where programmes differ in ways peculiar to the station, they communicate an alternative concept of the common good which relies heavily on the local community, a perspective the American station does not offer. If Alhurra succeeds in obtaining a serious audience, it will be among the upper class only. Yet the stations have more in common than they differ. Neither is commercially supported, and neither can claim to be unbiased: both explicitly seek to communicate a message funded by political considerations.

Endnotes

[1]Lawrence Smallman, *Rumsfeld Blames Aljazeera over Iraq* (4 June); available from http://english.aljazeera.net.

[2]Paul Cochrane, *Does Arab Tv Generate Anti-Americanism?* (26 June) Worldpress.org; available from www.worldpress.org/article_model.cfm?article_id=2002&dont=yes.

[3] Stacey Philbrich Yadav, "Of Bans, Boycotts, and Sacrificial Lambs: Al-Manar in the Crossfire," *Transnational Broadcasting Studies* 14, no. Spring (2005).

[4] This research was undertaken with the aid of several (Arab) researchers watching al-Manar between November-December 2004 and May-June 2005 in the United States, Lebanon, and Jordan. Alhurra was viewed in June 2005. Around 50 random street interviews were conducted in Lebanon and Jordan on both al-Manar and Alhurra during June 2005. I supplemented this qualitative research with numerous survey conducted on Arab media.

[5] I use the terms extremist and radical to describe, respectively, intolerant, rejectionist viewpoints and advocacy of the use of violence.

[6] The exact date of its founding is debated.

[7] Magda Abu-Fadil, "Al-Manar Tv: No Love for US But No Help from Taliban," *Poynteronline*.

[8] Ahmad Nizar Hamzeh, *In the Path of Hizbullah* (Syracuse, NY: Syracuse University Press, 2004).

[9] *Middle East International*, 24 June 2005, p. 13.

[10] Middle East Briefing, "Hizbollah: Rebel without a Cause?" (Amman/Brussels: International Crisis Group, 2003).

[11] Sami G. Hajjar, "Hizballah: Terrorism, National Liberation, or Menace?" (Strategic Studies Institute, US Army War College, 2002).

[12] Mona Harb and Reinoud Leenders, "Know They Enemy: Hizbullah, 'Terrorism' and the Politics of Perception," *Third World Quarterly* 26, no. 1 (2005): 189-90.

[13] Amal Saad-Ghorayeb, "Lebanon: Shiites Expres Political Identity," (Arab Reform Bulletin, Carnegie Endowment for International Peace, 2005).

[14] Graham Usher, *Dispatches from Palestine: The Rise and Fall of the Oslo Peace Process* (London: Pluto Press, 1999), 126.

[15] Julie Peteet, "From Refugees to Minority: Palestinians in Post-War Lebanon," *Middle East Report*, no. 200 (1996): 29.

[16] Julie Peteet, *Palestinians in Lebanon: Identity at the Margins* Journal of the International Institute, University of Michigan; available from www.umich.edu/~iinet/journal/vol3no3/peteet html.

[17] Peteet, "From Refugees to Minority," 29, Rosemary Sayigh, "Palestinian Refugees in Lebanon: Implantation, Transfer or Return?" *Middle East Policy* 8, no. 1 (2001).

[18] Usher, *Dispatches from Palestine*,126.

[19] Hamzeh, *In the Path of Hizbullah*,41.

[20] Center for Strategic Studies, "Revisiting the Arab Street: Research from Within," (Amman: University of Jordan. Principal Author: Mustapha Hamarneh., 2005), 78.

[21] Saad-Ghorayeb, "Lebanon."

[22] Oren Barak, "Commemorating Malikiyya: Political Myth, Multiethnic Identity and the Making of the Lebanese Army," *History and Memory* XIII (2001): 61-2.

[23] Ibid.: 64.

[24] Avi Jorisch, "Al-Manar: Hizbullah Tv, 24/7," *Middle East Quarterly* XI, no. 1 (2004).

[25] Jorisch, *Beacon of Hatred*,chap. 5, Avi J. Jorisch, "Al-Manar and the War in Iraq," *Middle East Intelligence Bulletin* 5, no. 4 (2003).

[26] Avi Jorisch, "Hezbollah Hate with a US Link; Subsidiaries' Tv Ad Money Serves an Odious Goal," *Los Angeles Times*, 13 October 2002.

[27] Avi Jorisch, *Beacon of Hatred: Inside Hizballah's Al-Manar Television* (Washington, DC: Washington Institute for Near East Policy, 2004), 67, 85.

[28] Magda Abu-Fadil, *Hezbollah Tv Claims Credit for Ousting Israelis* IPI Global Journalist; available from www.globaljournalist.org/archive/Magazine/Al%29Manar-2004q html. Jorisch reports that the annual budget of the station is $15 million. Jorisch, *Beacon of Hatred*,xiii.

[29] The most prominent satellite channels of these are the Christian-affiliated LBC and Hariri's Future station.

[30] Gérard Figuié, *Le Point Sur Le Liban* (Beirut: 2005), 478.

[31] Interview, official at the Lebanese Ministry of Information, 24 June 2005; Ibid.,486.

[32] Abu-Fadil, *Hezbollah Tv Claims Credit for Ousting Israelis*.

[33] Interview, Lebanese Ministry of Information.

[34] Jorisch, "Hizbullah Tv, 24/7."

[35] The only significant writing on the station is by the Washington Institute for Near East Policy, written by Avi Jorisch. Jorisch, *Beacon of Hatred*. His work is flawed in its overt bias. The author confuses callers and interviewees with the station's perspectives, and according to one analyst, takes many of his examples out of context. Interview with Professor As'ad AbuKhalil, California State University, Stanislaus, June 2005. Still, some of the core observations Jorisch makes are valid, albeit removed from their political context and symbolic meaning.

[36] Hisham Sharabi, "Arab Satellite Channels and Their Political Impact after the Iraq War," *al-Hayat*, 18 July 2003.

[37] "Hizbullah's broadcasting arms garner awards," Lebanon Brief News, *Daily Star* (Beirut), 12 July 2002.

[38] Jorisch, *Beacon of Hatred*,23.

[39] Interview, Lebanese Ministry of Information.

[40] Harb and Leenders, "Know They Enemy," 182.

[41] Walid Charara and Frédéric Domont, *Le Hezbollah: Un Mouvement Islamo-Nationaliste* (Paris: Editions Fayard, 2004), 171.

[42] Harb and Leenders, "Know They Enemy."

[43] Charara and Domont, *Le Hezbollah*,169.

[44] Ibid.,170.

[45] Hugh Dellios, "With an Eye toward Politics, Hezbollah Recasting Its Image; Savvy Tv Campaign Credited in Group's Battle with Israel," *Chicago Tribune*, 13 April 2000.

[46] Hamzeh, *In the Path of Hizbullah*.

[47] Ibid.

[48] Robert Fisk, "Television news is secret weapon of the intifada," *The Independent* (London), 2 December 2000.

[49] Jorisch, "Hizbullah Tv, 24/7."

[50] Hamzeh, *In the Path of Hizbullah*.

[51] Laleh Khalili, "Grass-Roots Commemorations: Remembering the Land in the Camps of Lebanon," *Journal of Palestine Studies* 34, no. 1 (2004): 17.

[52] "An Analysis of Arabic Press Coverage of the Iraqi Elections," Arabic Media Update, prepared by the Center for International Issues Research for OSD-Policy, 26 January 2005.

[53] John Lancaster, "Hezbollah Tunes In On Profits; Party's TV Station Airing US Movies," *Washington Post*, 19 June 1005.

[54] Al-Manar's web site, web manartv.org/html/enprograms.html.

[55] The station's transliterated name should be al-Hurra, following conventional guidelines, since "al-" is just "the." However, the station itself writes its name in transliteration as Alhurra. I follow their usage.

[56] Wendy Feliz Sefsaf, "Us International Broadcasting Strategies in the Arab World: An Analysis of the Broadcasting Board of Governors' Strategy from a Public Communication Standpoint," *Transnational Broadcasting Studies* 13, no. Fall (2004).

[57] Avi Jorisch, "Hezbollah Hate With a US Link: Subsidiaries' TV ad money serves an odious goal," (Opinion) *Los Angeles Times*, 13 October 2002.

[58] Congress of the United States, House of Representatives. 10 December 2002.

[59] "France clears Al-Manar telecast," aljazeera net, 19 November 2004.

[60] Caroline Drees, "Manar TV as 'Terrorist," www.washingtonpost.com (Reuters), 17 December 2004; "Al-Manar TV to go off Dutch platform," aljazeera.net, 17 March 2005.

[61] Lawrence Smallman, "Al-Manar and 'TV terrorism,'" aljazeera net, 21 December 2004.

[62] "Lebanon threatens TV ban reprisals," aljazeera.net, 18 December 2004.

[63] Smallman, "Al-Manar and 'TV terrorism.'"

[64] Yadav, "Of Bans, Boycotts, and Sacrificial Lambs."

[65] William A. Rugh, "Broadcasting and American Public Diplomacy," *Transnational Broadcasting Studies* 14, no. Spring (2005).

[66] Ellen McCarthy, "Va.-Based, US-Financed Arabic Channel Finds Its Voice," washingtonpost.com, 15 October 2004. Available from www.washingtonpost.com/ac2/wp-dyn/A33564-2004Oct14?language=printer.

[67] Lindsay Wise, "A Second Look at Alhurra: A US-Funded Channel Comes of Age on the Front Lines of the 'Battle for Hearts and Minds'," *Transnational Broadcasting Studies* 14, no. Spring (2005).

[68] Sefsaf, "Us International Broadcasting Strategies in the Arab World."

[69] Al-Hurra web site, www.alhurra.com.

[70] McCarthy, "Va.-Based, US-Financed Arabic Channel Finds Its Voice."

[71] Wise, "A Second Look at Alhurra."

[72] Sefsaf, "Us International Broadcasting Strategies in the Arab World."

[73] Wise, "A Second Look at Alhurra."

[74] Ibid.

[75] Ibid.

[76] Daoud Kuttab, "Al-Jazeera 'is run by Arab patriots,'" AMIN: Arabic Media Internet Network, 7 August 2004. Available from www.amin.org/eng/daoud_kuttab/2004/aug07 html.

[77] Paul Cochrane, "Is Al-Hurra Doomed? Lebanese Reaction to the US Satellite Station," Worldpress.org, 11 June 2004. Available from www.worldpress.org/article_model.cfm?article_id=1991&dont=yes.

[78] "Editorial Mocks New US Arabic Channel," *Al-Quds al-Arabi* (London), 17 February 2004. Available from www.worldpress.org/article_model.cfm?article_id=1927&dont=yes.

[79] Wise, "A Second Look at Alhurra."

[80] Rugh, "Broadcasting and American Public Diplomacy."

[81] Ibid.

[82] Ibid.

[83] Cochrane, "Is Al-Hurra Doomed?"

[84] "Al-Manar flays EU broadcast ban," aljazeera.net, 18 March 2005.

[85] Sefsaf, "Us International Broadcasting Strategies in the Arab World."

[86] Ibid.

[87] Sharabi, "Arab Satellite Channels and Their Political Impact after the Iraq War."

[88] West Bank and Gaza Presidential Elections, Final Report, European Union Election Observation Mission, 9 January 2005. Available from www.amin.org/eng/uncat/2005/mar/mar002 html.

[89] Jorisch, *Beacon of Hatred.*

[90] Islah Jad, "A road littered with disappointment," AMIN: Arabic Media Internet Network, 29 April 2002. Available from www.amin.org/eng/islah_jad/2002/apr29 html.

[91] Naomi Sakr, "Satellite Television and Development in the Middle East," *Middle East Report* (Spring) 1999: 6-8

[92] Cochrane, *Does Arab Tv Generate Anti-Americanism?*

[93] Wise, "A Second Look at Alhurra."

[94] Ibid.

[95] McCarthy, "Va.-Based, US-Financed Arabic Channel Finds Its Voice."

[96] Sefsaf, "Us International Broadcasting Strategies in the Arab World."

[97] Arab Advisors Group, "Credibility of Satellite News Channels in Greater Cairo."

[98] Arab Advisors Group, "Credibility of Satellite News Channels in Greater Cairo."

[99] Wise, "A Second Look at Alhurra."

[100] Cochrane, *Does Arab Tv Generate Anti-Americanism?*

[101] "Alhurra on the Cairo Street," Compiled by Summer Said, *Transnational Broadcasting Studies* 14, Spring 2005. Available from http://tbsjournal.com/said html.

[102] Center for Strategic Studies, "Revisiting the Arab Street."

[103] Ibid.

[104] Azmi Bishara, "Arab Valentine," AMIN: Arabic Media Internet Network, 18 February 2004. Available from www.amin.org/eng/azmi_bishara/2004/feb18 html.

[105] Sefsaf, "Us International Broadcasting Strategies in the Arab World."

[106] Jorisch, *Beacon of Hatred*,xvi-xvii.

[107] Wise, "A Second Look at Alhurra."

[108] Ibid.

[109] Rugh, "Broadcasting and American Public Diplomacy."

[110] Marc Lynch, "Assessing the Democratizing Power of Satellite TV," *Transnational Broadcasting Studies* 14, Spring 2005. Available from http://tbsjournal.com/lynch html.

[111] William Gamson, "The Social Psychology of Collective Action," in *Frontiers in Social Movement Theory*, ed. Aldon D. Morris and Carol McClurg Mueller (New Haven: Yale University Press, 1992), 68.